to all the women i've ever loved

ALSO BY BILLY CHAPATA

Chameleon Aura

Flowers on the Moon

Velvet Dragonflies

to all the women i’ve ever loved

BILLY CHAPATA

The authorised representative in the EEA is Simon and Schuster Netherlands BV, Herculesplein 96 3584 AA Utrecht, Netherlands. (info@simonandschuster.nl)

Andrews McMeel Publishing
a division of Andrews McMeel Universal
1130 Walnut Street, Kansas City, Missouri 64106

www.andrewsmcmeel.com

26 27 28 29 30 TEN 10 9 8 7 6 5 4 3 2 1

ISBN: 979-8-8816-0532-2

Library of Congress Control Number: 2025936881

Editor: Danys Mares
Art Director: Julie Barnes
Production Editor: Kayla Overbey
Production Manager: Julie Skalla

an ode to all the women i've ever adored: mother, sisters, friends, lovers

an homage to the divine feminine: creators, nurturers, intuitivists, goddesses

an appreciation for all the women who have taught me more about life, taught me more about myself, and taught me more about connection

an appreciation for all the women who have helped me grow, all the women who have helped me heal, and all the women who have helped me understand myself better

an appreciation for all the women who have stayed, all those who have left, and all those who have kept me in their thoughts and prayers to this day

you breathe life into all these pages, exist in all these words, and water all these sentiments

this is for her, this is for them, ***this is for you.***

CONTENTS

esprit.

and what i liked about her was that she saved souls simply by being herself.

her authenticity was medicine to the world.

(it's sad that she had to go through so much chaos to find peace, but it's also extremely inspiring that she found herself through it)

a double-edged sword, there was something truly impenetrable about the way she carried herself. her heart broke, but her mind did not crumble; her wounds split open on certain days, but her soul remained pure.

she was resilient,
she was strong,
she was stubborn,
she was pain,
she was joy,
she was life.

it will never be easy getting a second chance
with a woman who knows her worth.
she knows what she deserves too well
to allow you to break her heart twice.

things i've learned from being loved by a woman.

i. when a woman loves, her love never wavers. it remains
consistent and constant, even through dark and
troubling times; it remains solid and unbreakable,
even through the shakiest moments. it forms
a foundation in your heart built on truth.

ii. when a woman loves, her energy can be so powerful that
it rubs off on anything in close proximity, her essence
can be so enchanting that it attracts curiosity, her love
can be so strong that it overwhelms the presence of
everything and everyone around her, including herself.

iii. when a woman loves, her eyes never wander. the attraction
others may have for her is never strong enough to pull
her away from what her heart truly desires and
what occupies her attention; her commitment
can never be questioned, it never breaks.

waves.

a woman with intellect is beautiful, but dangerous.
the more you get to know her,
the more you discover;
the deeper you dive into her mind,
the more breathless you become.
she has the power to give you life
or to take it away
depending on how capable you are of swimming in her depth.

(she was a force to be reckoned with, even on her own)

you told me that you could never belong to anyone

and i grew to appreciate how divine that was about you.

your wholeness effortlessly existed within;
no one could ever complete you.

(expired bonds turn into lessons)

perhaps we jumped into things too fast, carried away by the smiles we shared and the laughter with which we filled every single room. perhaps we ignored too much, oblivious to our concerns and passive about our problems. perhaps we were in way over our heads, too young to understand love and too naive to realize that good connections go beyond attraction, chemistry, and desire. perhaps we didn't slow down enough to realize that *even good things require work.*

ego death.

we were just two naked minds
learning how to clothe ourselves in love,
but there was always
a deep ocean of misunderstandings between us.
maybe one day we'll be brave enough to drown our pride
so we can dive in and meet each other halfway.

immutable.

many lovers have slipped through your fingers like sand, like a truth you were never ready to hold. it was never your fault that you offered them all the jewels of your honesty, but they kept choking on their own insecurities. they've attempted to trap you in hands that can't hold your storms, they've tried to contain the depth of oceans you carry within you, to no avail. your growth intimidates them, your roots spread far too deep for shallow soil, but you see, *you were never too much—they were simply too small to understand the fullness of who you were becoming.*
so let them slip away,
let their absence be,
while you remain whole,
blooming
beyond reach
of those who cannot comprehend the beauty of your petals.

her vibe was attractive,
her mind was magic;
people thought she was stuck in her own little world,
but i liked the fact that all she cared about was her own happiness.

(trauma has a way of making it hard to recognize when you have a good thing)

i let the cracks in my heart
cast shadows on yours,
let my insecurities
become walls between us
when all you ever wanted
was to build a home.

i doubted myself,
but in doing so,
i started to doubt the beautiful things about you.
your love,
your patience,
the sincerity in the way you stayed
even when my fears tried to push you away.

i feel regretful now
for letting the splinters of my past
bleed into our present,
for making you feel like you had to prove
what you already gave so freely,
for questioning love
that only ever asked to be trusted.

you were always reassuring,
but i could never meet you halfway;
you were always open,
but i only closed myself off,
hiding behind fears
that were never yours to carry.

(continued)

i made you fight battles
that belonged to me,
and for that,
i owe you more than words.

i apologize
for letting my troubles
become the distance between us
when all you ever wanted
was to stand close.

an alchemist;

listen to how she laughs through the tough times,
how she produces sweet melodies from her lips
even in the worst moments,
notice how all the pain and burdens don't weigh her down.
she has the ability to find magic in every single situation.

misconceived.

i wish you knew that my lows weren't a punishment for you
but a bridge i had to cross to find my way back to the sun.

i wish you saw that silence can be a shelter,
not always a wall
stopping us from reaching each other during rough moments.

i wish your patience didn't falter when my spirit strayed from
its own light,
internalizing my actions as some fault of your own.

not every dark season needs a solution;
some only require
gentle attendance,
a soft presence in the room.

i wish you knew that i never asked you to carry my sadness,

only to understand that sometimes it kidnaps my voice and
occasionally makes me vanish into shadows, hoping i'll find a flame
to bring back to you.

enigmatic.

she could be hell on some days,
heaven on others,
sunny on some days,
gloomy on others.
you had to experience all sides of her to understand her beauty.

they will form all kinds of opinions for you prioritizing yourself differently now, create colorful assumptions about why you carry yourself the way you do, but remember, it's the ones who have no idea about the trauma and heartache you've endured to become who you are now who will always have the most to say.

(honest with many, vulnerable with few)

very few have seen her with no clothes on,
even fewer have seen her naked.

private party.

we were a quiet language, spoken in half smiles and glances, a secret script no one else could read. in crowded rooms, we moved like whispers in the background, holding hands under the table of expectation, turning everyone else's noise into muted static.

we created our own little world that no one else could travel to. in spaces filled with uncertainty, we understood each other beyond the confusion, finding peace in our private intentions and public disguises.

i loved that they never caught on,
that our love could never be decoded,
that we created a bond that couldn't be touched
by external opinion, validation, or judgment,
that we kept our connection sacred to us.

every woman has chapters in her soul that she lets few read,
deep oceans that she lets few swim in,
hidden mazes that only few have escaped.

divine detachment;

the thing about her is that she was happy alone. everyone around her was looking for a connection and something to grasp on to, but she was happy being free, she was happy being unchained, happy with no pressure of connections and love. she had an abundance of love flowing from within, and everybody else was just a distraction from everything she was trying to achieve. she understood herself more than anyone else understood her, and that was the most beautiful thing about her.

timeless.

she reminds me of '90s r&b and sun-kissed sunflowers.
she's the woman you can't get off your mind
and the woman you think of in the future.

(a story i kept to myself until today)

the flowers i sent to your doorstep got delivered to the wrong address, and with hindsight i'm glad that they did. you moved on quicker than i thought, so i doubt they would've made a difference, but i like to think that maybe i made a random stranger's day since i could never seem to get anything right with you.

murky destinations.

our love had the transparency of a morning fog, soft and thick, unclear beyond understanding, a cocoon we thought was warm but was only shadow. we held on to it tightly, confusing its weight for gravity, its pull for purpose.

the writing was on the wall
from the moment we first met,
and now i know that what we had
was never meant to last—
it was only meant to teach us both.

so we allowed it to fade away,
not as an act of loss
but as a call for clarity.

as the seasons slowly passed
and as the dust finally settled,
we finally saw ourselves for the first time
in broken reflections—
but not as halves of a connection,
as two people whole on their own.

you see,
unfortunately
love must crumble sometimes,
sometimes it must dissolve,
so that the mirror can finally reveal the truth:

we were always enough,
even without each other.

the greatest gift you ever gave me was the time and patience to hear me without judgment, and i hope that whoever you're giving an ear to now appreciates what i never got a chance to.

(when is it finally your turn?)

don't you ever get tired of giving out second chances?
in the name of love
in the name of family
in the name of sisterhood
don't you ever get tired of giving everyone else a chance
but never affording yourself a single one?

sour joy.

i'm sure that you're much happier now, unbound from the shattered
pieces that we both carried,
i hear it in the way your laughter fills rooms i no longer occupy.
it stung at first—

to know that my absence
could be your sunrise,
that your happiness could bloom
in gardens i no longer water,
but i learned to reduce
that pain with acceptance.

accepting that
you deserve to feel lighter,
to exhale effortlessly,
to feel free
without my shadows
lurking at your feet.

i know you're happier without me,
and i'm at peace with that now.

love doesn't need to linger
in the same shape it started in.
sometimes it's enough
to know that one of us
made it into the sun.

detached from distractions
and focused on her own path,
there's nothing more divine and dangerous than a woman
living in her purpose.

it was never your job to raise yourself, never your responsibility to teach yourself how to be a woman, but in a strange way, i'm grateful that you were able to learn so much on your own; *who you've become is wiser than any version anyone else could've imposed on you,* and it's beautiful.

fractures.

we met in a place where our shadows were louder than our voices, where our pasts sat heavy in our laps, refusing to let us rise into something gentle.

we tried to hold each other with shaking hands, fingertips stained by the ink of old stories we never learned to rewrite.

we wanted love to be a bandage, but it only pressed on open wounds. we were both so tired, clinging to fragments of wholeness, building a fragile shelter out of half-healed scars. in each other's eyes, we saw reflections of pain, not pathways to light.

it hurts to admit, but:
we were never healed enough
to be good for each other,
never kind enough to ourselves
to offer kindness freely.

maybe now we understand:
sometimes two broken pieces
don't make something more beautiful—
sometimes they just break more.

grateful that you gave up on me because it gave me
the room to take more chances on myself.

have you had bad luck with love,
or have you had fortuitous interventions
pushing you in a better direction?

—have patience, it will find you eventually

(it was everything you disliked about yourself that i loved the most)

it was the way your voice cracked when you got excited,
the way your hands danced when words felt too small to hold
your meaning.
it was the cadence of your laugh, offbeat, like a song that only
i could hear.

you carried yourself like you oozed oddities,
like you had impurities staining your spirit that couldn't be
scrubbed off,
like you had blemishes ruining your aura that couldn't be concealed,
but i found art in every single smudge,
i found poetry in your peculiar.

all the pieces that didn't line up
and all the flaws you tried to hide
were the places where your light
spilled out the brightest.

(it was always you)

you may have been out of your element briefly,
but *you never lost your magic.*
it was there all along,
just waiting for you to rediscover it.

duality.

she has a way of restoring your energy when reserves are running low, breathing life into your intentions when your patience is running out of air; *she has a way of reminding you of your power without stepping out of her own.*

self-reflection is a double-edged sword;
it allows you to hold a mirror to your soul
to show you what the rest of the world doesn't see.
it's a quiet deliberation within your own truth,
peeling back layers you thought were safe to hide behind.

it's a blessing
to be able to see yourself clearly,
to be able to sit with your flaws,
to understand the reason behind your wounds.
it's the key to growth,
to becoming,
to breaking cycles
that no longer serve you.

but it's a burden as well,
because once you become aware,
you can't ever unsee.

the weight of your own honesty
can feel unbearable sometimes,
like holding a flashlight
to every part of yourself
that you'd rather keep in the dark.

the sleepless nights,
the endless questions,
the wondering if you'll ever be enough
for yourself,
for anyone else.

the weight of knowing
how much work there is to do,
the fear
that you'll never reach your intended destination.

(continued)

self-reflection is
a beautiful battle,
a necessary ache,
because in the end
it's the only way to find yourself—
and even though it hurts in phases,
it's the kind of pain that finds a way to heal you.

(a woman you only had to experience once to remember forever)

crossed paths with you once and i've been trying to find roads back to you ever since.
regret is becoming a familiar address i visit every single time i think of you.

(the stamps in your passport won't solve all your problems)

you can find a momentary escape,
temporarily travel miles away,
but *you can never outrun yourself.*

nothing will change by constantly living in the past.
old doors won't open more quietly,
and broken windows won't pour light in any differently.
the pain that you carry won't lessen by resting
in the same beds that hurt you
just because they once brought you comfort.

(how many more times are you going to keep hurting yourself before you learn the lesson?)

have you learned anything from your heartbreak,
or are you still breaking yourself
in the name of love?
do you call it growth
when it feels like the same wounds,
just dressed in different clothing?

do you chase love,
or does love chase you away,
leaving you emptier
than when it found you?

have you learned to listen
to the cracks in your heart,
to the lessons whispered
in the calm after the storm?
or do you rush back
into the same fires,
hoping this time
they won't burn?

do you call it love
when it costs you your peace,
when it demands more
than it gives?

have you learned
that love doesn't have to hurt
for it to be real,
or are you still convincing yourself
that pain is just passion
in a different form?

i see you carrying the heaviness of hearts
that were never meant to be yours,
giving away pieces of yourself
that you can't get back,
but are you learning?

or are you still coming to grips
with the fact that love begins with you
and that breaking yourself
was never part of the deal?

you are never missing anything when you are actively working on yourself. that opportunity, that connection, that moment, *everything you deserve is on standby while you get yourself together.*

lone wolf.

some women thrive in community,
but you were different.
the more entrenched in solitude you were,
the more you stepped into your power.

self-mastery.

she spent intentional time sitting with her mind,
not as an enemy to be defeated
but as a wounded friend in need of understanding.
she faced her fears that were whispering lies,
the doubts that screamed louder than her dreams,
and the stories she told herself about who she could never be.

piece by piece,
she untangled the chains she had wrapped around herself.
the need for perfection,
the fear of failure,
the weight of expectations she didn't choose—
she let them fall,
one by one.

in conquering her mind,
she learned not to silence it;
she taught it a new language,
one of compassion, one of power.

she learned that the battle wasn't outside her
but within,
and once she won that war,
the game changed,
her world opened up,
not because it had been closed
but because she finally believed she was worthy of stepping into it.

she unlocked new levels of joy,
of freedom,
of possibility.

the doors were always there;
she just finally found the courage to turn the key.

her life didn't just expand;
it blossomed.
she moved like someone
who knew her power,
someone who understood
that *the greatest victory*
is learning to master yourself.

have you ever seen what love looks like up close? watch the way she waters herself and remains undeterred by anyone or anything that tries to take her off course, notice the way she plants herself in spaces where she feels growth and away from the absence of it—*this is love.*

you've apologized for being too much
too often,
you've apologized for not being enough
enough times already,
but *with the right ones, you won't have to diminish or minimize*
who you are
just to be seen or understood.
remember that.

expensive lessons.

you have so many receipts stored from times you went against your better judgment, and with time *i hope you learn to listen to your gut* so you don't have to pay the price for ignoring your intuition the first time.

(i didn't know what love was until i met you)

i was so wrapped up in my own world
that i forgot to take a deeper look into yours.
i naively saw love as something to take,
not something to give,
and in my selfishness,
i let all your needs fade into silence
while mine screamed out for attention.

you showed up for me
time and again,
pouring from a well
i never thought to refill.
i didn't ask,
i didn't see,
i didn't care for the weight you carried
because i was too busy
lightening my own load.

i apologize
for the times i left you empty,
for the times i mistook your patience for endless reserves,
for the way i let your needs
drown into the background
while mine stood center stage.

you deserved more—
someone who could hear you
without you having to scream,
someone who could give
without waiting to receive,
someone who saw you
and not just their reflection in your love.

(continued)

if i could go back,
i'd make space for you
the way you always made space for me.

you deserved reciprocity,
not an uneven tide,
and i'm sorry for being too selfish to see that love is about balance,
about giving,
about considering a heart
other than my own.

the complexities you would have to endure in trying to figure her
out was where her magic lay,
the mystery behind who she was is what made her attractive;
you could never put her into any kind of box to define her, and
that's what made her so beautiful.

(to one who shall not be named)

i love you,
but i love myself enough
to know better than to take steps back in my own journey to reach you again.
i wish you well, though.

that cycle has nothing new to teach you,
nothing to offer you,
nothing worth staying in it for.
resist repeating a lesson you've learned already
just because it feels comfortable.

(divine timing doesn't discriminate)

just because something finds you doesn't mean you have to keep it. be honest enough to admit when you aren't ready for that opportunity or connection, despite the impatience or loneliness; *if it's truly for you, it will find you again when your hands are in a better position to receive it.*

remorse.

you were a symphony,
and i was just learning to hear.
a masterpiece,
and i was still sculpting with shaky hands.
you stood before me,
a woman of depth, grace, and fire,
and i was not ready to hold what you were offering.

i wasn't prepared for the way you loved,
so fiercely,
so unapologetically.
i wasn't ready to match the strength
you brought to the table,
to meet your courage with my own.
i didn't know how to stand beside you
without shrinking beneath your brilliance.

i apologize
for making you feel like too much
when it was me who was not enough.
for trying to fit your infinite beauty
into the smallness of my understanding.
for holding back
when you deserved someone
who would leap into your depths without fear.

you deserved someone steady,
someone sure,
someone who didn't see your strength
as something to fear
but something to honor.

(continued)

in your leaving,
you taught me what it means
to lose something rare,
and now,
i carry the lesson in my heart—
to never stand before a blessing
and fumble what god has placed in my palms.

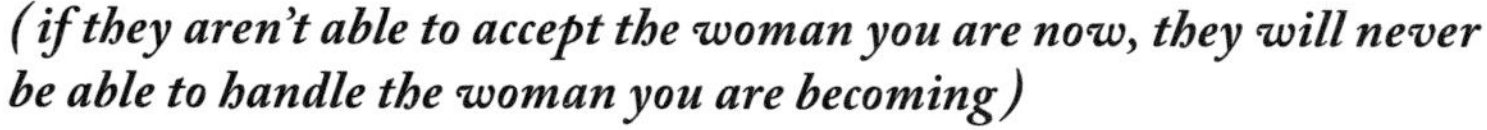

(if they aren't able to accept the woman you are now, they will never be able to handle the woman you are becoming)

you are not responsible for maintaining an image of yourself that people are comfortable with just because it is what they are most familiar with. you betray your growth every time you resurrect an expired version of yourself to appease anyone's ego.

bulletproof soul.

she was unstoppable when she was loved correctly
but
invincible when she poured the same intensity of energy
back into herself.

they will judge you for living in your truth.
for stepping outside the lines they've drawn for you,
for daring to be something they can't understand.
they'll label it selfish, call it reckless,
because your freedom reminds them
of the cages they've chosen to stay in.

they will create narratives of you,
not because of any wrongdoing on your part,
not because of any fault of your own,
but only because your authenticity
will make them question their own.

your light will feel too bright
for those who have been comfortable
living in the shadows;
your courage will feel like an attack
on their lack of vulnerability.

but look at their judgments
as a reflection of their insecurities,
not of your own.

keep living.
keep loving.
keep being everything
they don't want you to be
or what they said you couldn't be;

their opinions
will never matter more
than the peace
you find within yourself.

afterthought.

do you ever think about me
during moments when the clocks in your world slow down?

does my name ever color your mind
like strokes from a paintbrush that you can't ignore?

do i slip through any of your thoughts
like a scent in the wind that can't be caught?

do you hear my name
in the silence between your favorite songs?

because sometimes
you still bloom in my memories,
and i wonder if i grow in yours.

disappearing acts.

i noticed that sometimes she has to vanish
into the quiet of everything in her own world,
away from the noise,
away from the expectations,
away from everything that has stolen pieces of her.

it's not running—
but returning.

returning to the woman she forgot to be
while trying to be everything for everyone else,
returning to the woman she lost
while holding on to who people expect her to be.

she disappears not to escape
but to rediscover,

to sift through the rubble of her heart
and find the pieces
that still belong to her.

the world may not understand her absence,
but that's okay.
she doesn't disappear for anyone
but herself.

to learn how to catch her breath again,
to strip away the pressure of any roles and labels
that don't fit within her soul

(continued)

and when she returns,
she'll be lighter,
brighter,
and whole in ways they might never see

because sometimes,
the only way to be found
is to get lost in yourself first.

hushed avenues.

life has been a lot quieter since we parted ways,
but you'd be mistaken if you thought this was a bad thing;
i am grateful for the pathways to peace that your departure paved.

happiness is finding you again, the parts you thought would never heal are starting to feel less painful, memories that fogged the window to your soul are starting to clear, doubt that found resting space in your mind is moving out; *you are becoming you again, but even stronger.*

corpo.

she was attractive
not in the way her body or curves looked
but *in the way her mind and soul worked.*

it was never anything external that made me fall in love with you, but i guess that's all you ever knew. taught to hold your worth in how the opposite sex views you and not by your own standards, continuing cycles that the woman who brought you into this world was familiar with and never introducing you to new ways of thought. i don't blame you for who you became, nor do i hold any judgment or resentment; i just wish things could've been different. *perhaps your mother should've taught you how to love yourself first, instead of how to love a man.*

silent magic.

what made her powerful is that she let her energy speak for her.
she illuminated every room she walked in without saying a single word.

silent battles.

you've been in a lifelong battle with mirrors and holding yourself to unrealistic standards set by everyone else, and one day i hope you learn to *holster your weapons so you can see that everything starts with how you feel about yourself first.*

you have always been bigger than your struggles, even if they try to convince you otherwise. the world has managed to attach many lies to you, false narratives that wrap around your mind like chains, making you feel small, powerless, and unworthy, but they don't know the magnitude of your perseverance. no one has a clue of the storms you've had to walk through or the scars you wear now as reminders that you've been broken. every piece of you that fell apart, you gathered with hopeful hands and built back stronger; every tear that dropped to the ground watered seeds that now bloom in your soul—*you are not your struggles but the magic that overcomes them.*

(her glow would make constellations jealous)

a multidimensional being through her different phases,
she was the sun on some days and the moon on others,
warm enough for you to feel her presence even on her worst days
and bright enough for you to see her light even during
her darkest hours.

your essence was similar to trees,

grounded, unshaken, and rooted in something
deeper than the surface.
you carried yourself with the confidence
of branches reaching for the sun,
knowing that growth is inevitable
no matter how intensely the winds blow.

how you carried yourself reminded me of the way trees hold space,
never asking for permission to exist
but still able to offer shade, shelter, and solace
to those who need it.
you didn't demand attention;
you simply existed,
letting your presence speak for itself.

you possessed such steady energy,
like the way trees endure
in seasons of bloom,
in seasons of loss.
even when the world tried to strip you bare,
you stood firm,
knowing the cycle of renewal
would always bring you back to life.

how adaptable you were in your life added more color to your aura
reminiscent of the way trees
intertwined their roots deep within the soil,
connecting beneath the ground
to support each other selflessly
in ways invisible to the naked eye.

(continued)

your essence was similar to trees,

because like trees,
you didn't just exist;
you thrived,
you endured,
you flourished,
and in your authenticity,
i found a way to discover my own.

what do you do with your pain
after you've processed it?
do you lay it down gently,
like a heavy bag you've carried too far,
or do you throw it into the fire,
watching it burn,
letting the flames cleanse what it left behind?

do you hold it close,
as a reminder of what you've endured,
or do you let it drift away,
like smoke from a candle
you no longer need to light?
does it linger in your chest,
a quiet ache,
or does it dissolve,
leaving only the lessons it taught you?

do you transform it into something beautiful?
a story, a song,
a truth you tell to others
who are still learning how to let go?
or does it sit in the corners of your mind
like a faded photograph
you glance at but never frame?

what do you do with your pain
when it no longer attaches itself to you?
do you bury it in the past
or carry it forward
as a badge of resilience?
do you let it define you
or simply shape you
into someone softer,
someone stronger?

(continued)

because i've been wondering,
when the dust has finally settled
and your wounds have healed,
what happens to all the pain
that once felt inescapable to you?

do you let it rest,
or does it find a new place
to live inside you?

but you see,

you were built for much more than survival. you've walked out of wildfires unscathed, but that doesn't mean that will always be the case. sometimes you need to recognize the signs before the fire starts and go in the opposite direction.

(you're blooming quite beautifully)

i'm proud of the woman
you're growing into,
proud of how you draw strength
from wells that were once dry,
how you stitch grace
into every wound.

i've seen you hold heartbreak
with steady hands,
mold it into wisdom,
and create a stronger version of yourself.

you've learned to walk away
from anything that doesn't grow you,
to speak up for the parts of you
that were once living in silence,
to let your laughter sound
like a protest against doubt.

i'm proud of the woman
you're becoming,
proud of every boundary set,
every truth claimed,
every step toward light
you've chosen to take.

your becoming is a masterpiece,
and i'm grateful
to witness your unfolding.

she was everything that she thought she was,
that's the alchemy of a woman who truly knows herself.

you're one of one—

a masterpiece that has been untouched,
a rarity that no copy could ever replicate,
the way you move,
the way you speak,
the way your soul shines
like light through stained glass—
uniquely yours,
impossible to mimic.

there isn't a comparison,
no substitute,
no second version of you.
you carry the kind of energy
that feels like home
and an adventure
all at once.

you're one of one—

a constellation all your own,
lighting the sky
in ways no stars ever could.

they've tried to compartmentalize you
into things that make sense to them,
tried to package you
into hollow boxes,
but you were never supposed to fit into any of them.

you were always meant to stand apart,
always meant to stand firm in your truth,
always meant to remind the world
what it means to remain limitless.

no one else could ever
fill the spaces that you leave
or bring any of the colors you add.

you're one of one—

and that's more than enough;
it's everything.

envy.

i find myself missing you sometimes.
wondering what you're doing,
what you're looking at,
what scents surround the air in the place that you're in,
but in all honesty,
it's your tattoos i'm jealous of;
they get to be with you everywhere you go.

your support is the kind of beauty that doesn't need to announce itself—it just *is.* quiet, strong, like the roots of a tree that hold everything together while the branches stretch toward the sun. you don't stand in the spotlight; you become the foundation. you don't ask for credit; you become the reason i can take my next step. it's in the way you listen not to respond but to understand. the way you see me not just for who i am but for who i'm trying to be. you lift without making it feel like a favor, love without making it feel like a debt. *your support is a language of its own:* it speaks in small actions, thoughtful gestures, moments when your presence says more than words ever could. you have a gift of reminding me that strength doesn't need to be loud; it can be quiet and unwavering, like a hand on the back, holding you steady when you begin to fall. i've found a safe place to land in you, the kind of space that turns chaos into calm, doubt into belief, and encourages me to be the best version of myself.

youthful references.

her inner child has always been her muse—
a soft, uncut gem in a world
that attempts to make her forget
what freedom and authenticity feel like.

her inner child doesn't worry about perfection
or expectations.
she cares only about the moments that make her soul dance—
spontaneous laughter,
messy creativity,
love without fear.

when she doubts herself,
when she feels the mass of the world pressing in,
she closes her eyes
and sees that child staring back at her.

unbroken. unafraid. infinite.

her inspiration isn't in the future
or even in the present—
it's in the part of her
that has always known who she is
and refuses to forget.

you've always been my favorite flower,
watching you grow from afar,
adjusting to every season,
staying firmly rooted in your essence,
you've always been my favorite flower even if
we could never coexist in the same garden.

(i regret every single moment that i didn't love you in languages you understood)

i held the sun in my hands and dared to think it would never set.
i basked in your light, so sure it would always be there,
but i forgot to thank the warmth; i forgot to honor the fire.

i shouldn't have taken you for granted, but i did.
counting your presence as certain,
like the setting of the sun,
like the air in my lungs,
i let the comfort of your love
turn into complacency.

you gave me luscious gardens,
and i let weeds grow in them.
you gave me the sweetest melodies,
and i kept my ears shut tight.
you poured vibrant energy into me,
and i consistently ignored your cup.

but now, i see it all.

all the cracks in my reflection,
all the places where my selfishness
overshadowed your grace.

you deserved more—
more care,
more gratitude,
more of the love you gave so freely.

i regret the ways i failed to see you,
the times i made you feel invisible
when you were everything to me.
you were never an inevitability,
you were never just a fixture in my world;
you were a miracle i foolishly forgot to cherish.

if i could go back,
i'd hold you tighter,
love you louder,
choose you clearer every single day,
because *you weren't just someone to me—*
you were the only one.

it's beautiful how only a select few have access to you,
how you reveal yourself only to those
who appreciate your colorful petals.

discerning.

your cold exterior has them confused,
the mystery in your eyes has them lost,
their inability to figure you out has them assuming,
but behind the curtain, i know a much deeper truth exists:
you have so much love to give, but you haven't found a soul that deserves it.

(i hate that there was so much on your plate i didn't know about)

i can't help but think how much closer we would've grown if you were just a little bit more vulnerable with me, if you'd stopped hiding under so many masks to reveal the truth, if you'd stopped keeping so many secrets stored away in your heart, but i also understand why you did. to protect me, to keep my thoughts pure, to reduce any distractions i didn't deserve. but it doesn't hurt any less to know that you carried all those burdens by yourself when i was always here for you.

she has lived so many different lives,
but with every transformation she made,
she inched even closer into alignment with her authentic self.

welcome back:

it's good to see you happy again,
walking on your path with a smile again,
with more hope and assuredness,
sometimes it takes giving yourself what you need
to create a shift in your world,
and *i'm glad that you finally chose you.*

you have a museum full of wounds, but it is nothing to be ashamed of;

all the trauma you went through
artistically played a part
in the masterpiece you are becoming.

life has threatened to break you so many times, but each and every one of those times you've managed to rebuild yourself into something stronger. maybe the question isn't whether you're ready for the world, but whether the world is ready for you.

(the mirror can be your best friend or your biggest enemy)

if you're enough for yourself,
if the mirror looks back
and you're able to recognize the beauty
in your own reflection—
that's all that matters.

you've never needed their applause
to feel the music that lives inside you,
you've never needed their validation
to become the person you want to be,
you've never needed their approval
to know your worth.

be your own sanctuary,
build a home in your own heart:

the world's opinions shrink
into echoes you can ignore
when you recognize the magic
in you simply existing.

(every time someone left, she found more of herself)

there was a time when their presence felt like home—
but over time she realized
that she was shrinking in their shadows,
twisting herself into shapes
just to fit into a space that was never meant for her.

when they left, her world cracked wide open.

all the grief from people leaving came in waves,
but so did the clarity associated with it.
their departures left wounds,
but they also left room for something greater:
herself.

without their noise, she could hear her own voice again.
without their expectations, she could finally breathe freely again.

the emptiness that they left behind
wasn't really a vacancy at all—
it was space she needed to arrive
at herself.

she realized that her authentic self
had been waiting all along,
beneath all the masks she wore for them,
beneath all the compromises,
beneath all the fear of being too much or not enough.

their leaving wasn't the end;
it was only the beginning.

she arrived in her fullness,
in her power,
in her truth.
relieved
not because she was glad they were gone
but because she finally understood—
their departures
were the invitations she needed
to come home to herself.

lackadaisical lovers.

some people will only love you for your vessel because they are too lazy to see beyond anything on the surface, but you never have to allow anyone who lacks depth the time and space to explore the oceans that exist within you.

do you still keep people around
out of convenience?
do you hold on to hands
you don't really want to hold
because letting go
feels heavier than pretending to stay?
do you collect their presence
like dust on a forgotten shelf,
not because they add meaning
but because they fill the empty space?

do you let them linger
when their time has passed,
when their words don't reach you
and their energy feels misplaced?

do you keep their company
not because it feels right
but because you're afraid
of what the silence might tell you
about yourself?

do you still call it loyalty
when it's really fear?
do you confuse connection
with obligation,
telling yourself it's better than being alone?
or have you learned
that true love
can never bloom
in the soil of convenience?

(continued)

do you still hold on to people
who don't feed your spirit
just to avoid the ache of letting go?
or have you finally realized
that *staying out of comfort*
is the loneliest kind of company?

i saw the spark in your eye return once he left.
that's when i knew that the love he was giving you
wasn't love at all.

untimely.

i should've been there for you more often,
made myself available when you needed me,
given you enough room to reach me
not just in the moments when you were easy to love
but in the same thunderstorms that made you question
if anyone ever would.

i mistook your silence for invincibility,
but *even the strongest women need someone to hold them*
when the world becomes too heavy.

i wish i'd listened closer,
showed up sooner,
instead of assuming
you'd tell me when it was too late.

you deserved someone
who didn't wait for the breaking
to offer their hands,
someone who saw the rain coming
and stood beside you anyway.

i miss the comfort in your words,
the softness of your syllables.
your voice always sounded like a love song i had yet to write.

i guess

i was too caught up in the destination to appreciate the entire journey. too impatient to see that growth isn't a straight line but a spiral, a delicate dance of blossoming and breaking, a process that demands time, softness, and patience.

you were unfolding, a flower finding its light, and i was too blind to wait for the bloom. i wanted the beauty without the becoming, the finish without the fight. i failed to see that your growth wasn't a delay—it was a miracle in motion.

i feel terrible for the times you felt rushed because of my lack of understanding, for the moments i gave you the impression that your pace was not good enough. i should have been a place of comfort, a steady ground for you to place your feet, a safe haven for you to rest your worries, but instead i let my impatience shake the foundation of what we had already built.

you deserved someone who could sit with the messy parts, someone who could hold space for your transformation, and i was too focused on what you'd be to love you for who you were.

you were always enough. even in your unfinished chapters, even in your slow seasons, and i'm sorry for not having the wisdom to see that then. *you were growing, and i should have been patient enough to grow with you.*

(sometimes love isn't enough)

i'm still trying to forget the structure we raised from the rubble
of regret—
how we rebuilt ourselves,
stone by fragile stone,
only to find that our shelter
was shaped from broken promises,
immature intentions,
and hurried hopes.

life tore us down first,
it brought the worst out of us,
but then we gathered the pieces,
pretending like we knew
how to be whole again.

i'm still trying to forget the blueprint of us,
the architecture surrounding our connection,
the way we thought love could repair how damaged we were.

you deserve

connections that don't ask you to risk or jeopardize the balance of your nervous system just to keep them alive, connections that don't consistently send you to war with yourself just so you can find peace.

you've been glowing effervescently ever since you chose peace.
walking away from chaos was the best decision you ever made.

just like the moon,

you are not attached to darkness,
you are not married to any shadows that may stretch over your mind.
these heavy moments are just a chapter,
a mere intermission for you to finally catch your breath.

just like the moon,

your fullness will return again,
pouring hope into empty spaces within you,
smoothing the rough edges of your future,
preparing you for a brighter dawn.

just like the moon,

this phase will pass too,
and in its wake,
you will remember
that nothing stays heavy forever,
that light will always find a way in,
and that even the night bows to eventual glow.

but you see,

you were never broken. you were simply in a stage of rediscovery and reinvention, a phase of absorbing and unlearning, allowing the cracks to fall off while you slowly sculpt yourself into the masterpiece you have always wanted to be.

rules of accountability.

at some point, you have to look in the mirror
and admit the role you played in your own pain.

not because you deserved it,
not because it was your fault,
but because accountability is the only way forward.

you must acknowledge the moments
you stayed silent when your voice was begging to speak;
the times you excused the hurt,
hoping it would stop on its own;
the times you chose comfort over confrontation
even as the weight of it began to suffocate you.

yes, they hurt you,
yes, they should've known better,
but you had the power to walk away,
to draw a line,
to say, "this is where it ends."
and for whatever reason, you didn't.

this wasn't an act of weakness,
but it was certainly a lesson.

a lesson that you have to take accountability for
not as an act of blame
but as an act of empowerment,
because when you own your part,
you take back the pen,
you rewrite the narrative,
you stop being a victim of someone else's story
and become the author of your own.

it's never easy to admit
that you allowed it to continue,
but it's necessary,
because healing starts with honesty,
and growth begins
when you finally find the courage to say,
"i won't let this happen again."

i hope

with time you *find the courage to cultivate your inner world,* so when something good finds you, you are healed enough to recognize and receive it.

generational loops.

your mother's trauma
has been shackling you for too long,
her pain woven into the fabric
of your being
like a thread you never asked for
but can't seem to pull loose.

her wounds became your legacy,
her pain became your blueprint;
you've learned to carry burdens
that were never yours to hold,
mistaking them for love,
mistaking them for inheritance,
mistaking them for duty.

you walk through life
with mementos you didn't forge,
weighed down by stories
that weren't yours to write,

and you call it strength,

because that's all she ever taught you—
to endure, to survive,
to smile even when it burns—
but survival isn't freedom.

her scars don't have to be yours,
you can unlearn the hurt,
break the cycles,
let yourself be more
than what her pain allowed.

(continued)

you are not her past;
you are your own becoming,
and even though the weight is heavy,
it's not unbearable.

it's time to set yourself free.
for her.
for you.
for every part of you
that deserves to feel whole.

i pray

that you never let the wounded girl in you stop you from becoming the woman you've always wanted to be.

it was never another man's job to occupy the role your father failed to fill for you, and one day *i hope you heal enough* to realize that the search for someone to fill that void is only sabotaging your chances of finding true companionship.

ironic:

he's so opinionated about how you choose to live your life, but to rest in your femininity, you must first remember that some battles are simply not worth fighting. how could a man ever tell you how to be more of a woman?

some people will become so attached to unhealed versions of you that your growth will feel like a betrayal to them, but *it's not your responsibility to sugarcoat your transformation* so your changes are easier to digest.

black sheep.

you can't keep nursing old wounds like they're the only currency
your heart can afford.
you've told the story so many times, become fluent in the language
of pain,
forgetting that hurt
isn't a home—
just a place
you passed through.

there reaches a point where carrying the script of suffering burns
more than it warms, where
playing the victim dulls your own essence and makes you forget
that you can be your own hero.

cut the strings tying you to the past,
dismantle the chorus continuously whispering that you are powerless;
choose new words,
choose a new stage,
step into the light.
you've survived.

it's hard to build any kind of connection when you've never known what a stable connection looks like, but i hope your tomorrows become more tender than how rough the past has been to you.

vacancy.

emptiness steals so much, slipping in unnoticed,
taking up space in your chest
where joy used to reside. it's tempting to try to fill it
with everyone else's noise, with fleeting distractions, with
energy that almost feels right but is never quite aligned.

but emptiness isn't a puzzle for someone else to solve.
you can search the world, look for validation in every corner,
but the truth is, the void isn't theirs to fill, either. it's yours,
it's always been yours. no amount of hands holding you can
replace the way your own hands must keep your heart warm.

emptiness is a reminder—
a quiet nudge,
a gentle ache—
calling you back to yourself.

not to fix what's broken
but to sit with it,
to understand it,
to love it enough to begin again.

you are the one you've been waiting for,
no other soul can pour into you
the way you can,
no other person can light fires
that are meant to burn from within.

(continued)

the void doesn't need to be feared;
it needs to be filled
with your own tenderness,
your own truth,
your own love.
because in the end,

emptiness isn't a lack—
but an invitation
to finally become whole.

how long are you going to keep trying to attract the love you think you deserve before you realize that *you have to become what you want to attract first, before you are ready to receive it?*

intentionality.

take as much time as you need to heal,
take as much space as you need to occupy.
they don't need to understand your reclusiveness or your solitude
for the steps you make back to yourself to be meaningful.

are you not tired?

of betraying yourself
or silencing your own voice
to keep the peace for everyone else?

do you not ache
for the version of you
that you've abandoned
time and time again?

how many times
will you choose
their comfort over your truth,
carrying the guilt of your own needs
as if they are something
to apologize for?

are you not tired?

and if you are,
isn't it time to come home
to the person you've always been?

bloom unapologetically:

you are allowed to outgrow people, outgrow things, outgrow situations, without guilt, without shame, without explanation. you are allowed to become who you need to be without attaching an apology letter to every stage of your growth.

every time i thought she reached her final form,
she evolved into a version of herself that was even more beautiful
than the one she first introduced to the world.

she's done holding the weight of stories that aren't hers to tell,
carrying burdens that never belonged on her shoulders,
she's tired of being the glue for broken pieces she wasn't responsible for spreading.

she used to believe she was strong enough to carry it all—
but strength isn't about bearing it;
it's about knowing when to set it down.

and now,
her hands are free.

she no longer has the energy to carry wounds she didn't create,
she no longer has the patience to fight battles that aren't her own;
she's learning that love doesn't mean losing herself to save someone else.

she's choosing to let go of every single weight
that comes with guilt and unspoken obligations.

choosing herself
by understanding
that she was never meant to break herself
for someone else's healing.

she walks a lot lighter now,
and her heart is no longer a vessel
for pain that doesn't belong to her.

this is her peace,
her reclamation,
her refusal to carry
keys to anyone else's emancipation.

one day you will have to wash the blood off your hands from all the battles you've had to fight that weren't yours, and on that day, your healing will finally begin.

and here you are,

unlearning self-abandonment and relearning self-love, returning back home to yourself day by day, step by step, healing from the heaviness of old wounds that used to weigh you down. it was never too late to learn the lesson; *you have always been right on time.*

her laugh sounded like a soundtrack for freedom.
it was the melody of a woman free
from the clutches of anyone's opinion.

inimitable.

you could never replicate the aura of a woman who knows her purpose.
it runs deeper than what you see.
she's done soul work—
you can never imitate that.

how good it must feel

to know who you are;
to stand firmly in your skin
without apology
and without hesitation;
to look at yourself in the mirror
and see clarity,
not questions;
to carry the weight of your soul
like it's a gift
and not a burden.

how good it must feel

to know exactly what you want,
to chase your dreams with open arms,
and to walk down paths that feel like home.
to say "yes" with conviction,
and "no" without guilt.
to move through the world
with purpose,
unshaken by the noise around you.

how good it must feel

to be rooted in your truth,
to let your desires lead you
without fear of getting lost,
to trust the compass of your heart,
knowing it will always guide you home.

not everyone deserves to be a part of your transitional moments,
not everyone deserves a seat next to you during your growth,
there's a reason you're transforming into the divine feminine that you are,
and *not everyone will be compatible with her.*

a new era, a new start, a new beginning:

she told me that she was going to work on being her own biggest fan, because she spent too much of her old life being her own biggest enemy, and those words have stuck with me deeply ever since.

are you happy now that i'm gone?

did the silence bring you peace,
or does it echo louder
than you thought it would?

did the space i left
get occupied with something better,
or does it still hold the shape of me?

did you find the freedom you were chasing,
or does it feel heavier than my love ever did?

did my absence bring clarity,
or does it blur the lines
of what you thought you wanted?

are you happy now that i'm gone?

now that my laughter doesn't linger,
now that my touch is just a memory,
now that my heart no longer beats for you,
did the leaving feel as good as you imagined,
or did it take more than you were willing to lose?

i ask out of curiosity
because i left pieces of myself with you,
and i wonder
if they're at peace
or still aching
the way i do.

poisonous plots.

your jealousy seeped
into the soil of our love,
each drop a quiet toxin
clinging to the roots.

we tried to bloom,
tried to hold petals open
to the sun,
but the air got heavy
with mistrust.

it was never enough
to just be—
i had to prove, explain,
justify every branch i grew.

the plants in our garden withered away
with every pointed finger and accusation,
losing color and potential over time,
stealing any promise that we carried.

your jealousy managed to poison us,
turning soft ground infertile,
twisting stems into hard knots;

no flower can ever flourish
in an atmosphere
where it is choked tightly by suspicion.

there is no deeper betrayal than slowing down your bloom for someone who has no idea how much time you've spent watering your garden.

(even patience has an expiration date)

the air feels different now that i'm away from you. you see, *love breathes better when it isn't possessive,* when the energy in which it's cultivated is selfless on both ends, when you have the space to become your own person outside the connection, when it allows you to merge your individualities into one divine collective. unfortunately, you understood that too late.

(you have to be willing to meet yourself halfway
for our connection to grow)

we kept trying to stitch together the ripped quilt of us,
threadbare dreams and half-mended hearts.
you carried old ghosts into every hug we shared,
expecting my touch to somehow be the séance.

but *new love isn't a bandage for the wounds you refuse to clean.*

we can't grow together
while you bury your truths
beneath apologies you never followed through.

i can't be your redemption,
your quick fix,
your reassurance
that everything is fine.

you must meet yourself
in the mirror,
dig through the ruins
and rebuild your spine.

until you learn
to tend your own garden,
my love won't bloom in your soil.

we will always wither
in the shade of your silence
if you never learn
to shine light
on your own shadows.

i love you, but i love my peace a little bit more.

—sincerely, my regulated nervous system

(maybe if you focused on yourself, you wouldn't have time to envy my happiness)

there's never been any cold feelings on my end, never been a bone in my body that harbors ill feelings toward you, so *i hope you find healing one day.* resenting me for moving on with my life when you moved on before me is a heavy feeling to hold on to, but your regrets are not my responsibility to carry.

forgiveness isn't a doorway back into my life;
it's a window i vent to let the bitterness escape.

it's not an open invitation,
not a second chance,
not a reunion of hearts;
it's me finally being able to set myself free.

i can forgive you,
release the thought of what you did,
let go of the anger
that's been poisoning my essence,
but forgiveness isn't me forgetting—
it doesn't mean rebuilding
what was meant to fall apart.

i can wish you well
from a distance
and still lock the door to my peace.

i can honor the lessons
without welcoming the pain back in.

i can heal
and still choose a life
you are not a part of.

forgiveness is for me,
no one else.

it's how i reclaim my power,
how i close the chapter
without tearing out the pages.

(continued)

but *some stories end for a reason,*
and i've learned
that leaving you behind
is the final step
to moving forward.

i promise you

that one day my scars will be fluent in a much softer language,
whispering lessons instead of screaming wounds;
the pain you sowed deep into my memory will lessen its hold,
becoming loose under the weight of my healing.

i promise you

that one day i'll be able to walk past the hurt you left behind
like a chapter whose ending i already know,
gulping new air
that carries no lingering trace of your scent.

your absence
will cease to serve as an obstacle
but instead as a garden
where i learn how to plant kinder roots.

i promise you

that one day i'll stand in front of my own reflection
with no more heaviness
and no more sadness.

i will rise,
whole again,
filled with the warmth
of what i deserve,
and your name
will no longer be near my heart or my lips.

i am becoming more whole without you.
who knew all it would take was for you to leave
for me to feel complete.

rebirth.

i used to mourn who you used to be, how you used to carry yourself, the gentleness you possessed in your bones, but now i don't recognize you anymore, not even a hint of the girl i used to know. but maybe that's just what comes with transforming into a woman: *the birth of who you need to be even if it comes at the death of who you were.*

the grief of who you didn't become can consume you if you let it,
the grief of what didn't happen can envelop you if you give it space,
regret can handcuff your peace behind bars you can't escape if you allow it;
your transformation is always around the corner,
a better beginning is always close,
but first,
you must find love and gratitude for who and where you are now.

to whom this may concern:

you can choose whatever life you want now. you are not bound by the lies you were told to keep you less curious, not limited in how much you can stretch your wings to find better landing spots. you can choose whatever life you want now without feeling guilty for leaving behind who you used to be.

affirmation;

may we meet in another lifetime after we become the best and most healed versions of ourselves in this current one.

corazón.

they never tell you

that sometimes light burns out even if you're twin flames. perhaps our connection was never meant to last, but the lessons were meant to stay; perhaps there was a deeper reasoning behind our bond that goes beyond romance; perhaps the failure of our union was meant to encourage us to rediscover the fire that exists within us individually.

maybe it's not about finding someone strong enough to lift your heavy heart but about being light enough when you meet that person to not rely solely on them to lessen the load.

—healing

abeyance.

we met at a dusty fork in the road,
just two lost souls carrying heavy bags filled with questions
we never quite learned to answer.

our misunderstandings formed a horizontal line,
stretching into a future
where we wouldn't follow each other's steps.

our words were like traffic lights
in moments when we wanted to move forward,
constantly stuck on yellow,
with caution lingering underneath each breath.

you drifted right,
i drifted left,
and the air between us shook
with everything left unsaid.

we reached that crossroads
without a clean ending,
no neat ribbon to tie up the hurt,

but still
the world kept turning,

and *we had to learn*
to find peace
in an unfinished sentence,
to make sense
of what could never be resolved.

you were a poem that was always difficult to write, the kind that lingered on the edge of my thoughts, just out of reach, just beyond the tip of my pen. every word felt too small, every line fell short of your truth. you were the kind of complexity that demanded more than i was ready to give—a verse that wouldn't rhyme, a metaphor i couldn't quite untangle. i tried to write you in soft tones, but you were thunder. i tried to make you simple, but you were galaxies. every attempt to capture you felt like trying to hold water in my hands; you slipped through, free and untamed, refusing to be contained. you were a book that asked for more patience than i knew how to give, prose that required more honesty than i was ready to face, but now i see that *you were never meant to be finished.* you were meant to be felt, not defined; you were meant to be accepted, not for your existence to be questioned; you taught me how to love something without needing to understand it entirely, and even now, your lines remain unwritten, but your memory is etched into every part of my soul.

duplicity.

loving your mirror is such a double-edged experience.
how beautiful it is to find someone who relates to you,
how painful it is to see your own flaws within them.

we never needed anyone to validate our love. it was always ours—raw, unpolished, untouched by the perceptions of external eyes. we didn't fit into their clichés, didn't follow their rules,

but love has never been about regulations;
it's about truth,
and we had that.

they tried to measure us against their definitions, their versions of what love was supposed to look like, but how could they understand what they were never meant to hold? how could they judge what they couldn't feel?

our love wasn't a performance.
it wasn't for applause,
approval, or permission.

it was indescribable, unique, woven into the spaces only we could see.

we let them question it,
we let them misunderstand it.
their opinions were background noise that never touched us,
their ideas were too shallow to reach the depths of what we had,
because what we were was too deep for simple minds to comprehend.

perhaps

the downfall of our connection was us trying to be in control of
everything, not allowing things to flow, not letting certain things go,
not leaving space for growth. perhaps if we just gave each
other room to be imperfect, we would still be together today.

emancipation.

true love doesn't chain you, it frees you.
it doesn't shackle your growth out of intimidation—
it celebrates you.
it doesn't shrink your self-esteem out of insecurity—
it elevates you.
it doesn't keep a tight grip on you—
it gives your wings enough room for expansion.

some things fall apart not because you lacked will or worth
but because your angels saw the cracks forming long before you did.
some loves never bloom fully, some paths never straighten out,
some dreams collapse like old arches—all for the sake of your safety,
your uncharted growth.
it's easier to think of it as failure, to mourn what never took place.
but *sometimes an ending is a gentle hand guiding you away*
from what would eventually break you.
trust the method in the chaos, the pause between heartbeats—
your angels are at work,
carving a better way forward for you,
loving you too fiercely to let anything wrong ever last.

odd hours.

the love we shared between us transformed into a bright spark that lit up some of the darkest corners in my heart, managing to shine light and give warmth to parts of me that i had no idea were lacking. when we found ourselves in each other's presence, the world seemed to stop and the universe held its breath, but time has always been a cruel thief. it pulled at the threads of what we were, forcing us apart even as we tried to hold on. the love we had felt good, but in reality, it was clearly blooming during the wrong season. i think about you sometimes, not with bitterness, not with regret, but with a quiet ache, the kind that reminds me how rare it is to find someone who feels like home. you were that for me—but *home isn't always a place you get to stay.* maybe in another life, in another time, we'd get it right, but in this one, we were a beautiful story that couldn't survive the clock, and that's okay. some love isn't meant to last forever; it's meant to teach us what forever could feel like.

trajectories split as people grow. goals remain similar, but relationships change. regardless of the shifts you experience, you'll always know who is meant to be on your path with you because *they'll complement your journey instead of pushing you away* from your desired destination.

i wish i had been more honest with you,

naked with my truths
instead of disguising them in lies,
clearer with my intentions
instead of clothing them in ambiguity.

you deserved clarity,
not the shadows i surrounded you with.

i was convinced i was protecting you,
but i was protecting only myself

from the scrutiny of my own truth,
from the fear of what honesty might break.

so many nights you questioned yourself
when the fault was mine,

letting confusion linger
when i could've spoken light into the darkness,
letting doubt write my story
when courage was what you needed.

if i could go back,
i'd give you my whole heart,
unedited,
unfiltered;
i'd trust you enough
to hold even the messiest parts of me,
because you deserved that.

we went in expecting the worst from each other,
waiting to see who would be the first to break the other's heart,
anticipating disappointment because of how the past treated us,
but we were too naive to see that what we needed wasn't each other,
what we needed first was healing.

(by the time you realized that no one should have a say in our relationship except us, it was already too late)

your friends came with hollow buckets, pretending their words were concern, dousing sparks we tried to nurture. they told you i was too much, not enough, too restless to hold. their whispers seeped in like cold rain, cooling any warmth we had left. i watched as you listened, watched as you spilled doubt all over our foundation, watched as you questioned all the love we had built. the energy within our connection flickered out over time, drowned in opinions and judgments that were never ours to begin with. your friends poured water over our flame, and we stood there, dripping with regret, realizing too late that we let strangers extinguish our sacred fire.

overdue confessions.

maybe i should start with an apology, exercising accountability by taking full responsibility. i should've treated you better—by that i mean i shouldn't have taken you for granted. i should've been more honest with you—by that i mean i shouldn't have thought that lies could cover up the cracks in our connection. i should've known what i had when i still had it, but isn't that what every person says when they lose a good thing? so maybe this isn't really an apology, because that would be way too cliché. *maybe this is more of a realization,* more of an admittance of my shortcomings, my flaws, and my inability to love you in a language your heart truly understood.

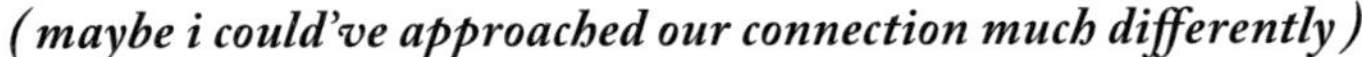

(maybe i could've approached our connection much differently)

you deserved more than counterfeit energy packaged as love—energy ripe enough to bite into during any season, energy with maturity dripping from its intentions—but instead it's my guilt that echoes in the hallways of our old connection. i've been navigating through karmic cycles, trying to rectify how i left things between us.

i have to admit,

i was never truly ready for the intensity of all your love. it flowed in like waves of lava, crashing over the walls i spent years building, pulling me into a depth i didn't know how to swim in. your love was fiery, wild and consuming, burning through my fears before i could even name them. i wasn't prepared for you to see me so fully, for you to hold me so tightly, for you to understand me without having to overexplain my existence. as much as i yearned for your love, i was afraid of its potency, scared of what it asked of me, terrified of what it might uncover. i never experienced love that demanded truth, so i ran. not because i didn't feel your love but because i did. i felt it in every dark corner of me, in every space that i thought was empty until you filled it. you deserved someone who was ready to hold your flame, not someone still learning how to hold their own.

out of service.

i awaited communication from you for so long, a text message, a call, an email, anything. not because i want to rekindle things between us but just so i could have confirmation that everything we had was real. *maybe your silence is all the closure i ever needed.*

even if we spoke today,

i wouldn't know where to start. wouldn't know how to explain myself for leaving our connection so abruptly, wouldn't know how to break down my thought process at the time. i dislike the person i was when i was with you because you knew what you wanted, and at the very least, you deserved someone who knew themselves.

you are the thing that my heart hasn't recovered from. the ghost that appears in my most quiet moments and the painting on the walls of my heart that refuses to fade. you've lingered around like a shadow, never heavy enough to crush me but always present enough to be a reminder that you were once here. i've tried moving to where the grass appears greener, tried burying any thoughts of you beneath time, beneath new beginnings, but nothing ever seems to sprout in the places where your memory still lives on. you're an ache i've learned to carry, a wound that doesn't bleed but never truly heals. i've rebuilt myself in so many ways over time, but you're the piece i can't seem to replace. you're the what-if that lingers in the back of my mind, the unfinished chapter i keep rereading even though i know how it ends. i've been telling myself that it's over, that i've let you go, but deep down my heart knows the truth—*you were a wind i never truly escaped, a fire that left a scar too deep to forget.*

yes, as a matter of fact,

when the moon comes out, i do find myself wondering about you
sometimes, wondering if i should return your messages, but then
i remember the teeth marks you left on my soul when we last spoke.
i will not be calling you anytime soon.

one of the hardest lessons you'll ever have to learn is that
having love to give doesn't entitle you to receiving it in return,
and not because you don't deserve it but because some people
won't understand or be able to handle the full capacity
of what you have to offer.

(some people teach you what love is; others teach you what love isn't)

i guess i should've known. i should've seen it in the way you spoke to me with words soaked in sweet softness but lacking any kind of real substance. you were art in an elaborate disguise, painted with rich colors that appeared vivid from afar but faded the moment i got closer. you were all charm, all glitter, but no gold, and i should've felt it in the brief moments of awkwardness between us, the way you left all my questions unanswered and my doubts floating heavily in midair. you never gave me clarity—only confusion wrapped in promises you never planned to keep. i should've recognized the weightlessness of your touch, how it never felt like home but a temporary place i was passing through. your affection was fleeting, like the wind—there for a moment and gone the second i reached for it, but i wanted to believe in you. i wanted to believe that the pieces you gave me were enough to build something real. i ignored the warnings, silenced the voice inside me that whispered, *this is not love.* now i know that you were never good for me, but maybe the lesson is what i needed to remember: that love doesn't feel like chasing, or questioning, or losing myself; it feels like staying, like growing, like peace—and you were none of that.

i will be grateful to you forever
because you taught me that you can't force someone to feel.
you taught me that you can't reciprocate what doesn't exist.
but above all,
you taught me how to love myself.

it was the idea of me that fascinated you. looking into the window of my soul from the outside, you saw something you wanted but weren't ready for. my appeal and charm wore off over time, and your intrigue came to an abrupt end. you got a taste of my reality, stepped foot into my world, but it didn't match the art piece you religiously created in your mind. *now you're just a stranger, and i'm just a prisoner of your infatuation.*

belated appreciations.

you held my love in your hands like it would never slip away, like it was sand you could keep, no matter how carelessly you let it fall through your fingers. you mistook my softness for permanence, my forgiveness for obligation. you thought i would stay regardless of how heavy the emptiness became between us, but love can never grow where it is taken for granted; it withers in neglect, suffocates under the weight of expectations never met. i gave you everything i had, but you looked past it, waiting for more—never realizing that there was so much more in your hands already. now, you're drowning in the memories of everything i gave you and haunted by the spaces i used to fill. but *your regrets aren't mine to carry;* they are simply remnants of your own choices, the consequences of love you never thought you'd lose. i've made peace with the lack of closure you left me with, i've grown within the emptiness that you housed me in, found light in the places you allowed to grow dim, and while you sit with the consequences of what you lost, i walk forward, unbothered, unburdened, knowing that my healing doesn't wait for your apology and my worth isn't tied to your remorse.

i hope you find what you're looking for,
but if you never do,
just know that i'll be long gone by then.

you loved me quietly—in little whispers, in the shadows, in spaces where silence felt safe. your affection tiptoed, softer than a breeze, barely disturbing the surface of my soul, but you wanted my love to be loud, to rise like a tidal wave and flood the world with proof. i wore myself down trying to make my love more noticeable, trying to paint the sky with feelings you only traced in pencil, but love isn't measured in the volume of its echo—it's in the weight of its presence. *maybe you never loved me at all,* you only loved the noise i made trying to reach you.

one-way ticket.

you finally saw my worth
when i had already packed it up,
when my heart had learned
to trust itself,
when i no longer needed eyes
that refused to see my light.

you finally believed in me
when i had stepped off the stage,
tired of overperforming
for an audience that
took me for granted for too long.

i was vulnerable enough
to introduce you to my dreams,
but you met every single one with doubt.

now that i've learned
to fly without your voice,
your sudden faith
feels hollow.

when you started to believe in me,
it was too late,
i had already found the courage
to believe in myself.

your applause now echoes
in my vacated heart,
but i've been gone for quite some time.

i feel silly for forgiving you and giving you so many passes for letting me down. perhaps it was my insecurity that blinded me, the lack of love for myself that poisoned me; *you were a lesson i had to learn* multiple times before i got the message.

i look back now and realize i carried so much that i didn't have to: misplaced intentions that were never mine to hold, burdens that never belonged to me. i let your doubts, anger, and unhealed wounds set camp deep inside my heart, bending myself backward to accommodate your chaos while consistently making excuses for every bruise you left on my self-worth.

but now i see it clearly:
i put up with much more than i was required to,
ignored the alarms that rang in my rib cage,
subdued my impatience to prolong the peace.

but my tolerance was not love;
it was self-betrayal,
a low vibration i no longer choose.

i am reclaiming the space
i gave so freely,
letting go of your pull
and your shadows.

from here on,
i am responsible for my peace,
no longer a casualty
of what you refused to heal
within yourself.

i still believe that you deserve goodness regardless of how you left things with me. i feel the regret in your words, i sense the heaviness in your self-deprecation, the sincerity in your apologies, and even though i can never carry a grudge, i can also never go back.

(the longer i stayed, the more i realized that what we had wasn't love)

i drank from your cup, not knowing the sweetness was laced with poison. you called it love, but it tasted more like control, it carried scents of confusion, it felt like a trap i mistook for safety. your love wrapped itself around me, not to hold me but to suffocate me. i didn't see it then, how every touch carried conditions, how every word was a load i couldn't bear. i thought love was supposed to hurt, because you convinced me that pain was proof of passion.

but now i know better.

love doesn't bruise, it doesn't cut, it doesn't leave you gasping for air;
love heals,
love holds space,
love doesn't demand
that you shrink to make it comfortable.

and still, i'm sorry—

for the part of me that stayed too long,
for the times i fed into the cycle,
for the moments i mirrored the hurt
instead of breaking free.

your love was toxic,
but i won't drink from that well anymore.

this apology is not for you;
it's for the me i forgot to protect,
it's for the heart i neglected
while chasing something
that was never truly love.

scarcity.

you spent so much time trying to prove that you
were worthy of my love,
and that's exactly why it never worked in the end;
you never truly believed that you were enough, even for yourself.

i hope

that you don't sabotage the next connection you indulge in by expecting the worst, sometimes beautiful things are meant to find you even if it feels too good to be true.

fall in love with yourself first,

before anyone can come along and shower you with their affection, before anyone can provide you with a resting space in their heart. you deserve to feel the warm embrace of your own energy so no one's presence or lack of it could ever leave you cold.

now that i think about it,
my biggest mistake was not that i tried to see the best in you
but that i thought i was flawed for having a big heart.

bittersweet.

there are pages of experiences we shared buried deep within my soul, but i struggle to write about you. there are plenty of languages our hearts spoke, but i struggle to talk about you. i struggle putting into words just how much of an impact you've had on my life, i struggle coming to terms with how someone who was so important to me can also be the reason for so many of the wounds i carry, i struggle finding the strength to carry the good memories when the painful ones keep weighing me down. but maybe *the lack of words is also a sign;* some things are just better left unsaid.

you hold a special place in my heart and always will,
but some special things are only meant to be admired from a distance
no matter how close up you'd rather be.

yonder.

i'm still rooting for you, even though you're not in my life anymore.
distance doesn't erase the care i have for you, doesn't undo the hope
i still carry for your dreams, for your peace, for your joy.

i cheer for you in silence now, a quiet love that no longer needs to
be seen to exist. i want your skies to stay clear, your path to stay
steady, even if i'm no longer walking beside you.

i'll never wish you anything less than everything
you deserve—healing, happiness, a love that reciprocates
what exists within you already.

my leaving doesn't mean i stopped believing in who you are or
what you can become; i'm still rooting for you, still sending
good energy your way, even if you'll never feel it,

because love like this doesn't need a audience—it thrives quietly,
in the spaces where goodbye never really meant an ending.

you kept the gate behind your heart closed so tight that you forgot you needed to let me in if our connection was ever to grow. the ironic thing about pain is that by guarding yourself from it, you can also hurt other people in the process.

i hope

you're learning to be softer with yourself since we last spoke, hope you're not being too hard on yourself for the mistakes you made, hope you're not carrying regret in your back pocket everywhere you go. you'll let yourself down many times in this lifetime, but that isn't a reason to stop trying.

you have been going to war for everyone's demons,
your family, lovers, and friends,
but, darling,
who has been fighting yours?

paternal wounds.

you are not your father's indifference,
not his closed fists of affection;
you are not the silence he used to fill the gaps
where love should have lived.

you have blood that boils with purpose,
a voice that aches to be heard,
skin stitched with resilience,
a spine carved from second chances.

you owe him nothing,

no apology for existing,
no validation of worthiness.

step out of the shadow he refused to light,
feel the sun on your bruised heart,
speak truth into every hollow moment,
learn the shape of your own tenderness.

he could not love you
as you deserved—
but that was never your fault,
never your burden to carry.

there is an entire world
beyond the absence
he built around you.

construct a life
in which you acknowledge your scars
without worshipping them,
and let every breath you take
be a testament
to the type of love you deserve.

illusions.

you've been so good at pretending to be strong,
so good at playing the role of protector,
so good at acting like nothing affects you,
but the wet mascara-stained pillows in your bedroom
always told me a different story.

your father broke your heart first, and then your mother made it worse by ignoring the damage he caused. *trying to pick up the pieces where others failed was my first mistake,* but we both had to learn the hard way.

you deserved better than the cold embraces
and clipped tongues,
better than the house
where tenderness hid behind slammed doors and silence.

you deserved voices that affirmed encouragement,
not insults etched into the soft places
of your soul.

you deserved laughter that felt like a lullaby,
not reminders of how little you belonged.

you didn't choose them—

they were assigned,
like a test you never studied for,
and you've worn their wounds
like badly fitting clothes,
outgrowing all the blame.

you deserved a family shaped by acceptance
and unconditional warmth,
a love that lets you unfold
gently.

they couldn't give that,
but their emptiness
has never defined your worth.

you can choose now:

love as a lighthouse,
friends as found family,
healing as your inheritance.

you deserved better,
but you can build it
with your own two hands now.

and if there's anything i hope you remember, it's that it's not your responsibility to fix me or anyone else—your friends, your family, strangers. *it's not your job to break yourself to make anyone else feel whole again.*

you were born into a hurricane you didn't create, a legacy of chaos written before you had a chance to speak. you learned to walk on broken glass, to find balance on uneven ground, to survive where love should have been the foundation. you shouldn't have had to suffer because of their unfinished stories, their unhealed wounds, their mistakes written into the script of your life. you deserved peace, but they gave you pieces, fragments of themselves you were never meant to fix. i see the burdens you carry, the quiet battles in your chest, the invisible scars on your skin. it wasn't your job to mend their fractures, to stand in the fire of their anger, to bear the cost of love that should have been unconditional. you were only a child, meant to be held, protected, and lifted, not left to navigate through the wreckage of a love that had sharp edges and didn't know softness. and yet, *here you are, not just surviving but shining.* you turned their shadows into light, their failures into strength, their mistakes into a testimony they couldn't be, but still, i'm sorry. sorry that they couldn't see your worth, couldn't meet you where you needed them most. you deserved better, and while i can't rewrite their part of your story, i hope my love can be the chapter that finally feels like home.

i hope

you learn to forgive yourself for thinking that your existence required an apology, for allowing anyone to place expectations on you without your permission. i hope you learn to forgive yourself for putting a mask on your authenticity to help anyone's projections breathe.

he loved the fact that you didn't know your worth because it meant he could control you, but if he truly loved you, the thought of you remembering yourself would never scare him; it would excite him.

you've been breaking your own heart for too long. occupying spaces that shrink every fiber of who you are, wearing disguises that mask your authentic self to make people comfortable, but *it's never too late to start clothing yourself in energy more fitting of who you want to be.*

heart fatigue.

you told me that you were tired of falling,

tired of the rush,
the butterflies that felt more like temporary fixes of dopamine
instead of something beautiful.

tired of the thrill that fades too quickly,
leaving you standing in the ruins
of another failed connection.

you grew tired of the introductions,
the rehearsed answers,
the surface-level exchanges
that never seemed to dive deep enough.

tired of building castles in the sky
only to watch them crumble
because the foundation was too weak.

tired of love feeling like a chase,
like a game with rules
you were never taught how to play.

you told me you don't want to fall in love anymore,
you want to *grow in love.*

something balanced,
something rooted,
something that doesn't feel like
you're losing yourself in the process.

i pray that it finds you.

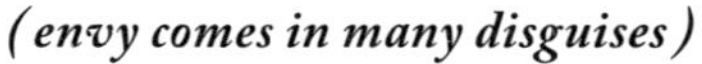

(envy comes in many disguises)

he sees your crown but would rather see it on his own head instead,
and i hope you remember that a lover in competition with you
doesn't love you at all.

people will keep showing you who they are until you decide
that the version of themselves they are consistently
showing you is no longer worth making excuses for.

is there such a thing as being too good of a friend?
if there is, that's all you were.
far too kind,
far too passive,
far too caring,
far too giving.
getting the bare minimum in exchange for your generosity
was never a fair trade.

how many times have you unpacked to people who pretended to clean the laundry you air out, only for you to notice dirt on your clothes when they're done listening to you?

—not every space is a safe space

darling,

sympathy is never a good enough reason to stay.

it feels honorable, doesn't it?
to stay because you care,
to stay because you don't want to be the one
to add to someone else's pain,
but sympathy is a hollow anchor—
it keeps you tied
but never truly connected.

you can't build a home
on a foundation of pity,
you can't call it love
when the only thing keeping you there
is the fear of what leaving might do to them.

staying out of sympathy
isn't kindness—it's avoidance.

avoiding your truth,
avoiding their truth,
avoiding the reality
that neither of you can thrive
in a space that's built on guilt.

they deserve more than someone who feels obligated to stay.
and you deserve more than to be weighed down by a sense of duty
that eats away at your joy.

sympathy can transform into stagnation
when it should be a strength,
delaying the inevitable
and calling it compassion.

but real compassion
is having the courage to walk away,
to free yourself
and let them find someone
who stays out of love,
not out of fear of leaving.

because staying for the wrong reasons
hurts more in the end
than leaving ever could.

(you have every right to be picky about who you allow into your world)

the softness you require is not something just anyone can show you, the healing your wounds need is not something just anyone can give you. for far too long you've been too casual with your heart, but understand that *there is nothing wrong with being selective about who gets to experience you.*

after how reckless the world has been with your heart,
here you are glowing,
growing,
still moving with love.
what a rebellious act.

understand

that your story hasn't concluded
simply because the chapter is ending.

turn the page with refreshed hope,
feel the edges, new with possibility,
remember that endings
are sometimes just pauses,
much-needed space to give your soul room to breathe.

you can still move happiness into
buildings where grief once lived,
find clarity in broken mirrors
that confused you before.

there are chapters waiting
to be filled with softer mornings,
kinder voices,
and a stronger version of you.

no pen drops here.
no curtain falls.
life keeps flowing,
and you with it—
holding the ink,
revising the cast,
formulating the next lines,
unafraid of what comes next.

to the passionate woman;

you've often found yourself struggling to convey love, the fire that burns within you doesn't have an on-and-off switch, your energy is so fierce that its intensity scares some away, but remember, you never have to settle for love that is not deep enough to swim in, incapable of giving oxygen to your flames.

to the reserved woman;

there is strength and wisdom in your quietness, power in how much they underestimate you, magic in your mystery. what you accomplish in silence is a testament to how dedicated you are to your dreams; your intentions are loud enough to drown away any of their misconceptions, and that speaks for itself.

to the misunderstood woman;

one day you will grow tired of overexplaining yourself, and on that day you will realize that the only person you owe an explanation to is yourself. there's nothing you can do about how people choose to perceive you, nothing you can do about what people choose to see in you, nothing you can do about the ideas people choose to project on you, but you can control how you choose to see your(self).

i hope

your future children meet a version of you who
no longer wears wounds as second skin,
a you who no longer tiptoes around scars like they're still fresh.
i hope they find a version of you who knows softness intimately,
who greets each day without fear,
who has pried open the rusted locks
of past hurt and aired out all the old pain.
may they learn strength from your astute example,
see that love can be gentle
and not a battlefield of apologies. may your laughter ring easier,
free of the ghosts that weighed it down before.
i hope your future children feel the warmth of a heart repaired,
the steady hands of a soul at peace.
i hope their inheritance is not your trauma
but your light.

her boundaries always served as proof that if you ever
wanted to reach her after you hurt her,
you would have to *go through god first to find her again.*

sometimes

you have to release what feels like love so you can create room for genuine energy to reach you.

gains and losses.

are you willing to lose connections to find more connection to yourself? to walk away from the hands that hold you back, even if they were once comfortable? are you ready to trade safety for clarity, to let go of the noise so you can finally hear your own voice? will solitude become your choice instead of settling, even if it does feel a little lonely at first? will you release the grip of relationships that no longer water your soul so you can grow in the ways you've always needed?

there's nothing straightforward about letting go of what kept you warm and choosing yourself over bonds that were keeping you tethered.

but *are you willing to lose it all*
to find something greater?

your truth,
your peace,
your wholeness?

because sometimes
the only way to truly connect
with yourself
is to disconnect from what isn't meant
to stay.

mind mesmerizing enough to get lost in,
intellect deep enough to drown in,
it's no wonder they're so intimidated by the waves you give off.

sell-by dates.

does it not
get exhausting for you?
carrying a heart heavier than stone,
dragging it through the days
as if pretending it carries no weight
will magically make it so?

you tell yourself to keep going,
to push through the ache,
but truth is,
your heart was never meant to bear so much.

it gets tiring,
holding on to pain that's past its time,
clinging to memories
that no longer serve you,
replaying moments
that only reprise the sting of regret.

you wonder why it feels heavier every day,
but you keep adding to your bag
without ever setting anything down.

it's okay to let it go,
to stop carrying the guilt,
the anger,
the sadness
you've tucked into every corner
of your heart.

it doesn't mean you're giving up;

it only means you're giving yourself
more of a chance to feel light again.

she's given grace more times than her heart could count, more times than the world thought she should. not because she didn't feel the pain but because she knew that *holding on to bitterness would only drown her.* she's given grace to those who never asked for it, to those who never deserved it, not because they were worthy but because *she* was. she didn't want to carry the heaviness of animosity in her spirit, didn't want her heart to harden under the weight of resentment, so she chose grace, every single time, even when it hurt, even when it stung, even when it meant letting go of apologies that would never come. *she extended forgiveness not as an offering to them but as a gift to herself.* she's given grace more times than most would, and that's why she walks lighter, peaceful, glowing, because her heart is a garden, and she refuses to let grudges grow there.

luminosity.

you never changed how brightly you emitted your light.
even when the world threatened to dim you,
even when your energy was drained by certain situations,
you showed up beautifully every single time,
in every single phase.

love has always existed right beneath your feet.
meet yourself halfway;
you'll discover that *it was always you.*

mweya.

she was magnetic,
one with god,
one with the universe.
everything she attracted was a result of all the hard work she put into herself.

divine offerings.

it was a blessing every time i stood inside your orbit;
every word you spoke became a soft place for my heart to land.
your laughter carved paths through my shadows,
turning my doubts into quiet echoes.
in your company i remembered tenderness,
how good it felt to be known without question.
my scars sang in melodies instead of cries when your
existence surrounded me,
my fears loosened their grip, and my soul found warmth
in your presence.
i still carry those moments like notes stored on a shelf
in the back of my mind,
grateful that i even got the chance to experience your light.

she's the type of woman stripped of coincidence.
if she ever comes into your life,
know it's for a divine reason
and because *god is looking out for you.*

(thank you)

you'd probably never admit this to me because it wouldn't be in your character to take credit, but i know i made it through some of my most turbulent moments because you kept me in your prayers, i know you had conversations with god about me and held me in high regard during my lows, i know you spoke goodness and healing into my life every chance you got. i could never thank you enough for being medicine when i needed it the most, for being an angel in human form, *for being you.*

constantly evolving.
every time they thought they understood her,
she added a new color or texture to the art piece she already is.

who you're becoming will only be palatable to select souls,
your growth will be an acquired taste for the ones also doing
the work, the changes will be digestible only to those with the
depth to understand what you bring to the table;
this version of you comes with new standards.

digital mirage.

i know it must be difficult to be a woman in a world that bases its merits of validation on likes, reposts, and comments. your beauty and depth are minimized by people's perceptions of image and the social construct that media has impressed upon us all. people can't quite grasp the other layers that make you the truly unique and divine woman you are. they can't see how vast your mind is by looking at your body, they can't see how intellectual you are by looking at your face, and they can't absorb your true essence just by seeing the outer characteristics you encompass. *you are much more than your body, your face, and your curves.* you are a goddess with so much more to you, and i hope you never forget that.

you're art; they don't have to understand you.
you weren't built to validate their opinions or cool their insecurities.
be accepted for the beautiful ambiguity you are.

you have a way of making clouds vanish from my world so the sun can appear just by hearing your laugh and seeing your smile, and i thank the stars every day for your existence.

i found you in the sun, in the way it rose every morning,
faithful and warm, reminding me that light exists.
even after the darkest nights, you were there in its glow,
in the quiet promise of a new beginning,
a quiet strength that asked for nothing but gave everything.

i found you in the moon, soft but still,
guiding me through the darkness when i couldn't see my way.
you were the calm reflection of light,
gentle but powerful, reminding me that even in my shadows,
i was never alone.
your energy changed in phases, but it was always there,
just like the moon.

i found you in the stars, scattered in the sky,
each one containing traces of your divinity that glimmer in the night.
you showed me that there is beauty in everything
that couldn't be touched,
to continue trusting in the magic of what simply exists.

i found you everywhere,
but i didn't just find you;
i found myself too,
in the light you reflected,
in the darkness you revealed,
in everything that existed within the universe.

i manifested so much goodness with you by my side,
attracted so much light with you in my presence.
calling you a good luck charm would be doing you a disservice;
you were a goddess in human form.

precedence.

they say she's absorbed in her own essence; i say it's beautiful that she is. it's beautiful that she's focused on her own journey, it's beautiful that all she's concerned with is her growth, it's beautiful that she doesn't follow the crowd and moves to her own tune. she's a free spirit, going with the wind, and if you can't keep up with her, *that's not her fault.*

woman,

many will be fascinated by you, but very few
will be equipped to understand you.
it's a gift and a curse to be someone with so much depth.

you have so much to offer this world. probably more than you realize, probably more than you've allowed yourself to believe. it's in the way you're able to show up on the days that make you feel invisible. it's in the way your kindness ripples, even when you think no one notices. it's in the way your light shines, even when you feel surrounded by shadows. you carry something unique, a gift no one else can give—your voice, your perspective, your energy, all so important. you've lived through storms that would have broken others, yet here you are, still standing, still offering pieces of yourself to a world that desperately needs them. you don't have to be perfect, you don't have to have it all figured out. what you offer isn't about grand gestures or loud declarations; it's in the small things: the way you listen, the way you love, the way you make someone feel seen when they need it most. *this world would be less without you.* so never hold back, never shrink yourself. step into the truth of who you are, because what you bring to this life is something only you can give.

she was multidimensional,
she liked hip-hop and astrology,
she got lost in the melodies, but she belonged to the stars.

potency.

there's something powerful about a woman
who is comfortable in solitude,
a woman who doesn't need the presence
of another soul to feel whole,
a woman who loses nothing in her own company,
a woman who still manages to exist with or without you.

soft light

she didn't have to force her energy on you to be felt,
or steal someone else's to be seen. she had a way
of illuminating your existence just by being.

(years later, and i still feel your energy on my skin)

your energy was
uncontainable,
uncontrollable,
electric,
constantly charging the air between us
with something pure and rare.

it was a language
i wasn't remotely familiar with
until you entered the room,
and suddenly every cell in me
understood your frequency.

you were a once-in-a-lifetime experience,
a solar eclipse of the spirit and the soul,
a divine cosmic alignment
that was far from ordinary.

there was no handbook
to holding this much grace,
no instructions for cherishing a moment
that burns so bright.

i still feel the vibrations
where you once stood.

some energy passes through
and leaves you changed forever.

you were that miracle,
that brief brilliance
i'll spend a lifetime remembering.

it's when your soul had no makeup on that i
found you most beautiful. when you were vulnerable,
authentic, and honest. i miss those deep conversations.

expensive habits.

if i could go back,
i would do things differently and sip a lot slower this time;
a few tastes of you and i was never the same again.

(passion comes in different forms)

her words were smooth and sweet on some days
and hard to swallow on others. she was like a
spoon full of honey with a shot of vodka.

we flew up too high,
way too fast,
like shooting stars
without a map.

we forgot
that gravity exists,
that *love needs slow breaths*
to anchor it down.

if we had tasted each moment
instead of devouring it,
we might have let softness
define our tempo,
we wouldn't have rushed
past any red lights of doubt,
crashing into walls
we never cared to notice.

unfortunately,
patience was the lesson
we skipped,
the song
we never allowed
to become our theme.

maybe if we had moved slower,
listened more,
been more intentional,
we could've built something steady
instead of something
that eventually fell apart.

we tried to hold each other like puzzle pieces that just wouldn't fit, smoothing corners, pressing edges, ignoring the gaps that carried quiet truths. we wanted to call it love, as if naming it would be enough, but the closeness we chased never settled into our bones. it remained a sigh, an almost, a fragile illusion that kept slipping through our cupped hands. you can't make a rose bloom by yelling at it to unfold, you can't force tenderness where honesty doesn't live; *intimacy can't be faked,* and neither could ours, no matter how deeply we wanted to feel less alone.

(we were made for each other, temporarily)

perhaps when we first met, we were both broken.
perhaps our scars are what attracted us to each other.
perhaps we saw so much similarity in one another
that we couldn't resist each other's energy.
perhaps this was a *divine plan to help us find worth in ourselves again,*
and now that we have found that,
we have no use for each other anymore.

i could never look at us crossing paths with each other as a coincidence, even if our time together was temporary. you taught me things that i will carry with me forever, *even if i had to hurt to learn the lesson.*

sometimes,

people grow apart, with no malice in the energy, no resentment attached, no overdrawn explanations, just distance. sometimes your paths split in two different directions and your journeys become incompatible with each other despite what existed before.

if the connection is not reminding me of my magic
and is not reminding you of yours,
why are we even wasting our time?

and maybe we could've gone the distance,

if only our words had found each other
instead of getting lost
in the spaces between us.

i spoke,
but you heard something else.
you spoke,
but i filled in the blanks
with my own fears.

we were just two hearts,
beating in sync
but speaking in foreign tongues.

our silence grew louder
than our intentions,
our pride grew heavier
than our love.

if only we tried to listen—
not to respond
but to understand.
if only we had met in the middle
instead of standing at opposite edges,
waiting for the other to leap.

love was never our problem.
but love can't survive
without clarity,
without effort,
without two souls brave enough
to lay down their armor
and simply say,
"i see you. i hear you. let's try again."

we could've gone the distance,
but instead
we stopped short—
not because we didn't love
but because we didn't know
how to speak the same language.

our connection tasted like quick relief, like a momentary hush in a room crowded with worries. we reached for each other, not because we were whole but because we were both falling and wanted something, anything, to slow the speed of the descent. it wasn't healing, only a pause, a borrowed breath before the tension returned. it wasn't love, just a quiet place to hide from the noise within ourselves. we held on so tightly and tried to make a home out of our makeshift sanctuary, hoping it would become more than an escape. but comfort is not a cure, and rest is not resolution. *we were never the answer to each other's emptiness*—just two lost souls resting in the same void.

my mother always told me to trust in god's timing,
so imagine my shock when i found god in you
but we still couldn't find a way to be together.
love can be cruelly ironic.

you resonated so deeply with me and managed to build a whole language that spoke to my spirit, but not every soulmate can be a lover, not every soulmate can be romantic, and even though we tried everything to make sense of our compatibility, *we were never meant to be more than platonic.*

she was the type of woman you had to take in small doses
because *her aura was so addictive.*

i was too young in my soul, too naive in my understanding of what it meant, to hold a love like yours. i thought love was about catching it, about owning it, about making it mine, but i didn't know it was meant to be free. i was too immature to see that love doesn't demand or take; it simply flows—soft like a stream, steady like the sun. because you see, love isn't about being enough for someone else; it's about being whole enough to let them be themselves, and i wasn't there yet. but i'm learning, and i hope you know, *you were never the lesson; you were the blessing.*

you deserve

softer hands that are able to receive your heart.
i am still learning how to hold a good thing,
and it was never your job to teach me how to do that.

home has been gone ever since you left.
not the walls or the roof,
not the space i return to every night,
but the feeling,
the warmth, the comfort,
the knowing that i was safe.

you were home
not because you stayed
but because you made me feel like i belonged,
your presence was a place i could rest,
a shelter from the storms i never had to face alone.

even surrounded by familiarity,
i feel untethered in my own life.

i've tried to re-create home before
but it's never the same.
the silence feels colder,
the laughter replays too loudly in my memory,
every corner seems to whisper your name.

it's interesting how someone can take so much with them
when they decide to leave,
not just the tangible things
but the essence of what made life feel so whole.

you see,
you didn't just leave—
you took the meaning of home with you.

now,
i'm learning to rebuild.
i'm trying to find a new sense of belonging,
even if it's just within myself.

on some days,
i wonder if home will ever feel like home again,
or if it will always feel
like a place awaiting your return.

it's probably for the best that there's been distance between us, but you still appear when i shut my eyes, boarding planes in the astral to see me when i least expect it, making an appearance to remind me of your existence. i've always wondered if it's still considered no contact when you decide to visit me in my dreams.

do you regret anything from our last conversation?

any of the words that stuck to your tongue
for far too long
or the ones that you let spill out
without much thought?

do you replay it
like i always do,
wondering what could've been different
if we had just chosen softer tones
and gentler truths?

do you regret the silence
that stretched between us,
thick with all the things
we were too afraid to say?

do you wish you had stayed a little longer,
listened a little deeper,
or is it easier
to leave it as it was—
unfinished,
uncertain?

i wonder if you hear my voice
in your slower moments,
if the echoes of our words
still bounce around your mind.
do you wish you had said more
or less?

(continued)

do you regret the way we let goodbye
feel so final?
because i do.
not just for what we said
but for what we didn't,
and i can't help but wonder,
do you ever sit with the aftermath of that moment
the way i do?

misdirection.

i don't think our spirit guides liked the idea of us being together, otherwise we would've been in each other's arms again. we had sweet moments, but we were also destructive in each other's presence. when our energies flowed, it felt heavenly, but when we crashed, it was chaos; *perhaps we were both being protected from each other.*

i'm grateful that things never worked out between us,

relieved that our journeys took a detour
before we got caught up
in a lifetime of wasted potential.

we could've continued to linger in illusions,
floating around in each other's emptiness,
pretending to be whole,

but the universe certainly knew better,
rescuing us from a lesson
we were too stubborn to learn.

i'm grateful that your absence
became a catalyst for my growth,
that your departure allowed me
to grow my own pair of wings,
that our flame burned out
before it engulfed everything that remained of me.

it's never upset me that things between us never worked out;
i'm just thankful for the freedom to find myself
in the aftermath of everything we had,
steadily learning how to love myself
without settling for less
than i deserve.

the magic between us died,
but the memories continue to live on.
what a bittersweet realization.

i've been searching for you in everyone since you left,

in their laughter,
i listen for the similarities to yours,
but it never quite fits;
their joy feels borrowed,
like a melody trying too hard to harmonize with my memories.

i look for you in their eyes,
but they don't hold the same depth,
don't carry the same storms and sunsets
that used to make me feel seen,
even when i didn't know how to see myself.

i trace their words,
hoping for the warmth of your voice,
the way you could speak
and make the world feel lighter,
but their sentences always fall flat,
missing the density of substance
only you were able to give.

i've been searching for you in their touch,
in the spaces where intimacy should feel familiar
but doesn't.
their hands don't carry the same tenderness,
the same understanding and knowing
that made me believe i was home.

i search for you everywhere,
in strangers, in moments,
in places i shouldn't.
and every time,
i come up empty,
not because they aren't enough
but because you're still everywhere
i haven't let go.

i don't know if it's you i miss
or the way i felt when i was with you,
but i've been searching,
and no one else has ever felt
quite like you.

one of the most painful lessons i'm having to learn is that i have to be brave enough to let you make your own mistakes no matter how much i love you. i could never babysit your discernment and gatekeep you from what you need to learn even if i wanted to.

savior complex.

you can't save anyone from themselves. you'll try, though. you'll pour yourself into them, thinking your love will be enough to heal the wounds they refuse to tend. you'll offer your light to people who are determined to sit in the dark, and you'll wonder why they don't move, why they don't see the hand you've been holding out for so long. but the truth is, some people aren't ready to be saved. some people cling to their chaos like it's the only thing that's ever been theirs. you can't rescue someone who doesn't want to leave the fire, you can't carry them out when they're too busy fueling the flames. it's not your job to liberate anyone from their plight. it's your job to love them, to support them, but also to know when to let go, because saving someone should never require losing yourself. they have to choose their healing, they have to want it, fight for it, step into it on their own terms. all you can do is be a mirror, showing them what's possible—but they're the ones who have to believe it. and when you realize that, when you stop breaking yourself to fix other people, you'll finally find peace. *saving someone isn't love; letting them save themselves is.*

are you really happy with him?

does he make your heart skip
the way you once said i did,
or is it a quieter kind of love,
one that settles instead of ignites?

do you laugh with him
like you laughed with me,
or is it different—
softer, safer,
but missing the spark
we used to hold?

does he see you
the way i did?
all of you—
the light, the shadows,
the parts you hide
from the rest of the world?

does he hold your fears gently,
or does he brush them aside
like they don't matter?

is his love enough
to fill the spaces i left behind?
do you ever look at him
and see pieces of me,
or is he everything i couldn't be?

are you really happy with him?
not the kind of happy
you show the world,
but the kind that sits in your chest
when the lights go out?

because if you are,
then i'll let this question
fade into silence,
but if you're not,
then maybe, just maybe,
you'll think of me.

i pray

that you fall in love with your life again, that you remember what it's like to wear happiness as a fragrance, that doubt removes itself from your soul's dictionary, that you find routes that lead you back home to yourself.

understand

that i don't need you to be my peace;
i just need you to know peace
so we can both recognize chaos
before it threatens to disrupt how we show up in this connection.

she's taking time to heal not because the world demands it but because her soul does. she's stepping back not to hide but to mend the places that feel torn. she's choosing herself, finally, in a way that feels foreign but necessary. on some days, she feels weightless, like the past is just a shadow she's finally outrun. on other days, it will come back heavy, a storm she must sit through. but she's learning to be patient with herself, to trust the ebb and flow of her emotions. she's taking time to rest, time to breathe, time to sit in silence and hear what her heart is asking for. she's pouring into the parts of herself she neglected while chasing things that never filled her. she's realizing that *healing isn't about rushing for relief* but about embracing every part of the journey. she's not there yet, but she's closer than she's ever been, and for the first time, she's okay with taking her time, because when she rises again, she'll be wiser, and she'll be unstoppable.

you've been angry at the world for too long now,

carrying that fire in your chest, letting it burn you from the inside out. you've made a home out of the rage, called it your armor, your shield, but don't you see that it's only been weighing you down? life can be unfair sometimes, but you've known that for too long. it can be cruel and chaotic, asking more from you than it ever gives back, but your anger won't change that. it won't heal the wounds or rewrite the past, it won't bring peace, only exhaustion. you've been fighting everything, everyone, even yourself, and maybe it's time to put the sword down. not because the world deserves forgiveness but because *you* do. you deserve a life that doesn't feel like a battlefield, you deserve mornings that don't carry the stench of yesterday's wars, you deserve to let go of the fire before it consumes everything good inside you. it's okay to be angry, it's okay to feel it, to sit with it, to let it remind you of what matters, but it's not okay to let it define you. you are not your rage, and the world doesn't deserve the power you've given it over your peace. it's time to let it go. not for the world, but for yourself.

you've been angry at your family for too long now,

carrying the heaviness of their mistakes, their words that cut too deep, their love that sometimes feels like control. you've held on to the pain like it was proof of your strength, like letting it go would somehow mean they didn't hurt you. but the truth is, your anger has been a prison, though not for them; they see no fault in their actions, living their lives in whichever way they wish. the prison is yours, built brick by brick from resentment and confusion. you deserved apologies that never came, love that didn't come with conditions, understanding that wasn't earned through tears or heartbreak, and it's okay to be angry about that. it's okay to feel the ache of what should have been, but you've been holding on to it for too long now. it's not healing you; it's keeping you stuck, tethered to a version of yourself that's still hoping they will change. maybe they never will, maybe they're still learning, still figuring out how to love in a way that doesn't hurt, and perhaps that's not your burden to wait for. letting go of the anger doesn't require forgetting, doesn't require excusing; it means freeing yourself from the grips of the past, it means choosing peace over pain. you've been angry at your family for too long now, and it's time to let the load fall, time to stop carrying what's not yours to fix, time to make space for the love you deserve, even if it has to start with loving yourself.

you've been angry at yourself for too long now,

carrying the fragments of every mistake, every misstep, and every moment when you think you should have known better. you've been replaying the past like a punishment, as if holding on to the guilt will somehow make it right. but what good has it done? what has your anger built other than walls around your heart? you've made a habit of beating yourself up for things you can't go back and change, and it's exhausting, isn't it? living every day as your own worst enemy. you forget, you're human. you forget, you've been learning, growing, trying your best even when the world didn't give you much to work with. you've held yourself to standards no one else could ever reach, and when you fell short, you turned that disappointment inward. but you don't deserve this. you don't deserve to carry this anger, this shame. you don't deserve to live your life feeling like you're never enough. it's time to forgive yourself not because you're perfect but because you've suffered enough. let it go. let the anger fade. not because it's easy but because it's necessary. you've been angry at yourself for too long now, and it's time to choose love—love for the person you were, love for the person you are, and love for the person you're still becoming.

you're no ordinary woman, and you've done the shadow work, so don't let it surprise you that other people aren't able to comprehend your magic. you are a version of themselves they haven't been able to meet yet.

your boundaries cost you so many friendships, but they also saved you so much time, and even though i can see how lonely it occasionally gets, i can also feel the relief that comes with not having to release energy into spaces that aren't conducive.

you are love with or without them.
their absence or presence could never take away
from what exists within you already, and *that is your magic.*

unbreakable promises.

she carries all her yesterdays
in the curve of her spine
but proceeds with grace
that defies the disasters she's endured.

she wears her truth like armor,
shimmering with scars that
once silenced her laughter.

now, she smiles—not for the world
but for the child inside her,
the one who patiently waited
for love to come home.

she builds a life that feels
gentle, warm, and safe,
where shadows are just reminders
and not threats.

her authenticity is her offering,
her joy a revolt,
her peace a revolution.

every tear she wipes,
every breath she reclaims,
is a promise fulfilled—

a vow to never let
her inner child
feel unseen again.

you've spent too long grieving connections that you thought were meant to stay, been stuck on old chapters, mourning versions of you that no longer exist, but you deserve to become whoever you want without the past holding you back;
allow the space for a beautiful rebirth.

your inner child is clapping softly,

in the quiet corners of your heart,
beaming with eyes wide open
at the person you've grown into.

they see how you carry yourself,
with a stronger spine, steadier breath,
less afraid of the world's sharp edges.

speaking a more authentic language,
treating softness like a treasure,
letting your laughter roam free
in places where silence once lived.

your inner child is proud,
smiling in that secret dialect
only the two of you understand,
recognizing the courage
it took to climb out of old stories
and write a new script,
one where you are loved,
safe,
and
beautifully yourself.

she's a prayer you never knew you made
until you finally got to experience her.

swoon.

grateful for them,
grateful for her,
grateful for you.

regardless of whether the experience was bitter or sweet,
regardless of whether the lesson was difficult or smooth,
regardless of whether the outcome was exhausting or beautiful,

i'm grateful
for the person you were,
the person you are,
and the person you're becoming.

when some women are divinely placed in your vicinity, it's much
deeper than coincidence, and
now i know that without you, i wouldn't be who i am today.

from all the languages in my mind,
all the poems in my heart,
all the energy in my body,
and all the stories in my soul—
merci, obrigado, gracias, ndinotenda, *thank you.*

ABOUT THE AUTHOR

billy chapata is a zimbabwean writer, artist, and creative based in atlanta, georgia. he immigrated to the united states during his late adolescent years, but writing has been a staple for him throughout his entire life. having lived in various countries ranging from china to kenya, chapata's exposure to different cultures allows for deeply informed thoughts and writing that reflect on a wide spectrum of experiences. touching on topics of healing, self-love, and growth, his work aims to help people find a way back to themselves through poetry-infused words and sentiments.